Candy Quotes

Craig Williams

For Claire, Megan & Harry

© 2007 by Craig Williams
Revisions and additions

ISBN 978-1-84799-768-5

INTRODUCTION

The quotes in this book come from the minds of some of the thousands of people who have ordered printed tshirts through the website tshirtcandy.com.

Having run tshirtcandy for over 5 years, and printed thousands of tshirts, I am still surprised, shocked, amazed and amused at the words people choose to have emblazoned across their chests. So much so, that I began to compile a list of the ones which stood out (for one of the above reasons) and have finally brought them together in this book.

This book, therefore, is an insight into the minds of these people and the messages about themselves that they wish to get across. Whilst some of the quotes will amuse or startle you more than others, don't forget that each and every one was placed prominently across the front (and occasionally back) of a tshirt for all to see. Quite often chosen just to cause a reaction.

Perhaps in these pages you'll find a message that strikes a chord, or a philosophical gem that you take to heart. Whatever you take from it, I personally believe it is a showcase for standing out from the crowd, for being unique, and having the courage to display your message to all, proudly. So enjoy and be inspired!

Craig Williams

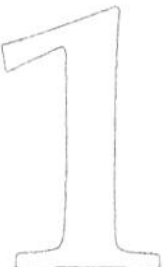

Numbers

0 to horny in 2.5 beers

"24 hours in a day, 24 beers in a case. Coincidence?"

4 kids through university - and I'm still the smartest one!

"40 years, wife, 3 kids, a mortgage... How would your hair look?"

665 neighbour of the beast

90 hours a week and loving it

2

A

A boy named Sue

"A pint of "cuddles" please!"

"A pub – ahh yes. A meeting place where people attempt to achieve advanced states of mental incompetence, by the repeated consumption of fermented vegetable drinks. "

Accept that some days you're the pigeon and some days you're the statue.

Acts 16:31 believe on the Lord Jesus Christ and you will be saved.

Addicted to girls

"Ah, but you have heard of me"

Ailerons have landed!

"Alcohol, the cause of and solutions to all of life's problems"

All the dude ever wanted was his rug back… it really tied the room together

All those who believe in psycho kinesis raise my hand

Also in sober

Am I meant to care?

Am not the best looking guy in the world… but 'ave got a crackin' personality

And in the beginning God said "Oi, John, how much to light this place?" So I did Him a deal.

Angel in training

Anybody come at you yet?

Apathy is catching

Aphrodisiac

"As you grow old, you lose interest in sex, your friends drift away and your children often ignore you. There are other advantages of course, but these are the outstanding ones"

Ask me about my vow of silence...

Aspire not to have more, but to be more

Available for hire

Awesome vegetarian

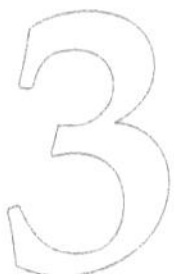

B

Backs are for stabbing. Mine being the exception that proves the rule.

Barristers do it on a trial basis

"Be bold, go for the old"

Be unique and different. Say yes!

"Been there, done that, got the t-shirt."

Behind every successful woman is a substantial amount of coffee

Better than Barbie

Bionic grin

Blame it on a simple twist of fate

Blow it all

"Bomb disposal technician, if you see me running try to keep up"

Born to bitch

"Born to shop, forced to work"

Brad & Jennifer 2000 - 2005 (shame): Brad & Mandy 2005 - forever (much better)

Buy me for £2.50. Membership plus great new benefits!!!!!!!!!

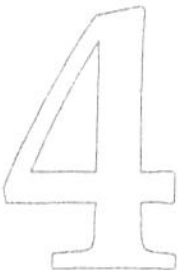

C

Can you read this?

Candy bar

Can't even think straight

Carparklife

Caution. Risk of death. Keep clear. Do not obstruct

Caution: Contents doesn't do mornings!

Cheap people write crap code

Cheeky monkey

Chlamydia can be caught… but cromulence can't be taught

Chocolate muffin? Cheers very much!!

Christmas kiss examiner… first examination free

"Claire likes charity shops, but not your face"

Classy not trashy

Cleverly disguised as a responsible adult.

C'mon the hoops!

"Cocaine, me? God forbid…"

"Coffee, chocolate, men. Some things are just better rich!!!"

Come to the dark side. We have cookies

Communists use metric

Creativity is great; plagiarism is faster

Creep up on me Darren

9

Ctrl+alt+Del

Ctrl+alt+Del

5

D

Damn right I've been naughty... Now spank my evil butt

Dance? Disco? Yeah... I'm good!

Dark chocolate + sunny days + cuddles + green rabbits

Definitely not gay!

Designed for your pleasure

Dignify me with immanent critique

Dip me in amyl nitrate and throw me to the gays

Dip me in chocolate and throw me to the lesbians

Diplomatic immunity

Do not arrest this man

Do not invade my personal space!

Do you always read the small print?

Do you have to open graves to find girls to fall in love with?

"Do you promise to funk, the whole funk, nothing but the funk?"

Does this colour match my hair?

Dolphins are just gay sharks

Don't ask me… I just play bass

Don't criticize your government

"Don't cry because it's over, smile because it happened"

Don't forget I'm the boss!! Yeh I know

Don't hate me cos you ain't me!

Don't look at me… I'm shy!!

"Don't mess with me, I'm a librarian"

"Don't talk to me, I only open my mouth to change feet."

"Don't talk to me, unless you're Brian May"

Don't tell me the West Ham score!

Don't touch the bump

Don't waste your time asking… I can't be arsed

Don't you wish your boyfriend was Hoff like me?

Drama queen

Drink till I look better!

Drink… till you want me!!!

Drummer and rock climber - I drum with altitude

13

"Dude, we're going to Ibiza!!"

Duracell badger

6

E - F

Easy world

Elephantly waisted

Escaped mum

Everybody loves a girl who can bake... I've got a bun in my oven!

Face ache

Fancy a sausage?

"Fancy dress? Err... No, I would rather die!"

Fat but rich

Faux git

Feel the rhythm....

Fetch me a jar… coz I'm pickled!!!

"Fire up the ovens, muffin man! We got a big order to fill."

Flypaper for freaks

"Forget gravy, love custard"

Friendly local megalomaniac billionaire

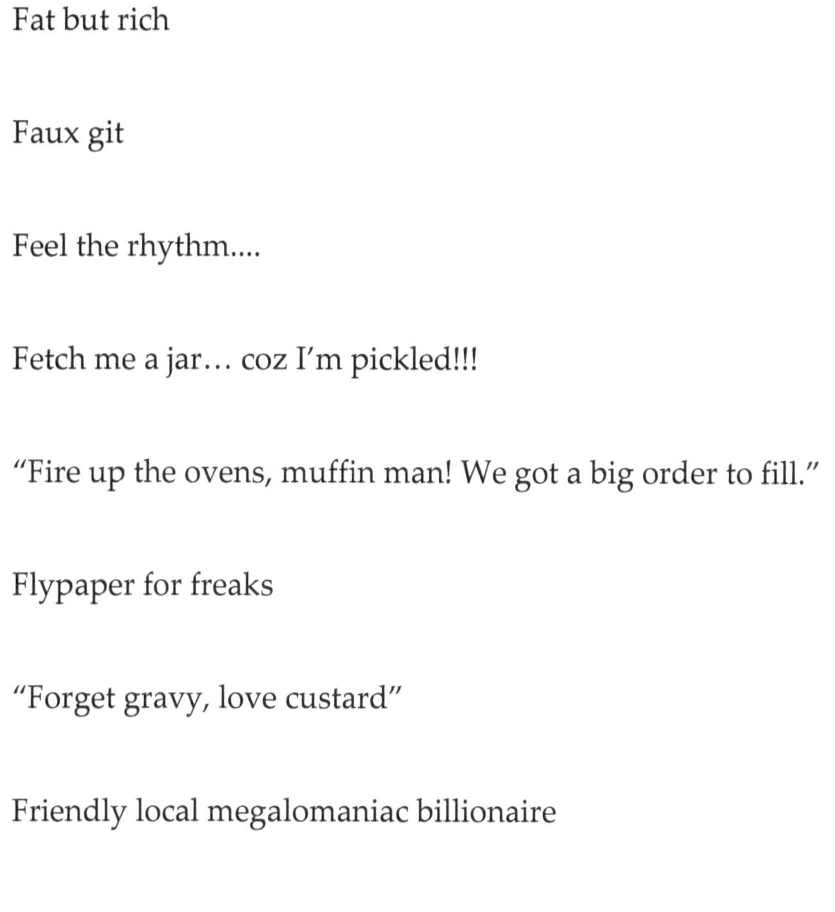

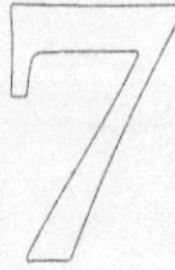

G

Geek bird

Get in the queue

Get me drunk and enjoy the show

Get off my train!

Giddy up a ding dong

Ginger beer

Giraffes are evil

Give in to your wrong side & let's get dirty!

Go back to art school

Go on... open your prize

Gobi desert canoe club

God is a single parent too!

God must love stupid people as he created so many...

Godlike creature

Groupie

Gullible idiots welcomed

Guns don't kill people. Americans do.

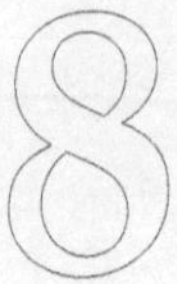

H

H is for horse

Hand mash

Have a go… and see how far you get

Have you seen the muffin man? Damn b*stard owes me $5

"Hello, hello, is there anybody out there?"

"Hello, I'm Johnny Cash"

He's not my boyfriend

Hey you guys!!!

His way up

Honk if your vector field is divergence free

How am I?

'How long is too long to leave custard?''

Hughes the daddy?!

I

I don't play well with others!!

I am a miserable b*stard

I am 18. Yeah you heard!

I am a legend in my own mind

I am away from my computer

I am not rude. You are just insignificant.

I am smirky for a reason...

I am Spartacus

I am the Stig

I am the victim here

I ate all the pies because... Fat guys are harder to kidnap

I came out the closet & all I got was this lousy t-shirt

I can only please one person a day and today isn't your day!

I can't handle this heat!

I caught you a delicious bass

I could be a friend to you

I could be a friend to you

"I could be at home tucked up in bed or watching Eastenders, eating bacon sandwiches and Thai sweet chilli crisps."

I did it because you said I couldn't

"I didn't ask to be a princess, but if the crown fits!"

I didn't get where I am today by saying earwig instead of thank you

I don't have Tourette's... You're just a c*@t

I don't mean to put it out there but... who's your mate?!

I dream that I am chemical

I engaged in industrial action and I must be punished!

I friggin' hate pink

I had a party for two with Shania Twain

I hate t-shirts with ironic slogans

I have nipples Greg... could you milk me?

I hear voices... and they don't like you

I knew I'd married Miss Right but didn't know her name was Always!

"I know I'm drinking myself to a slow death, but then I'm in no hurry."

I know I'm in love… cos I forgot the biscuits

I licked a llama!!

I like big butts and I cannot lie!

"I like my sex the way I play basketball, one on one with as little dribbling as possible"

I live my life a pint of beer at a time

I love animals (they are delicious)

I love Britney spears…and I'll fight anyone who says otherwise!

I love that song

I may be butch… But I will always be Angel Face Baby Cakes to my ma

I miss my ex boyfriend but my aim is improving

CANDY QUOTES

I put the 'sexy' in dyslexia

I put the stud in study

"I read about the perils of drinking, so I gave up reading"

I read your blog all the time.

I read your email

I reject your reality and substitute my own

I rock more than a boulder!

"I rock so much, even ninja think I'm cool."

I said 'no' to Claudia Schiffer…

I see dead pixels

I see dumb people

I see your lips moving but all I hear is blah blah blah…

I spent most of my money on beer and women. The rest I just wasted.

"I started off with nothing; I still have most of it left!!!"

I suck at this game

I support Man Utd but I am seeking help

I taught Anthea Turner everything she knows!

I taught your boyfriend that thing you like

I thought port was a drink

"I used to be schizophrenic, but we're okay now."

I wanted a dog and I got this thanks to my responsible Aunty Val!!

I wear black on the outside because black is how I feel on the inside

I wish this shirt was blue

I wonder why u stare at me every time I put on this shirt!!!!

I would quit this job but I need the sleep

"Idaho? No, you da ho!"

If a job's too hard it's not worth doing

"If all the worlds a stage, I want better choreography"

"If I can't bring down heaven, I'll raise hell"

If I'm lost please return me to Graham

If I'm wearing this t-shirt then it's time for bed…

If it doesn't kill u it makes u stronger.

If it's grockle season why can't we shoot them?

If meat is murder... Is Quorn wasting police time?

If you c4n r34d th1s u r34lly n33d to g37 141d

If you can read this I've lost my cape

If you can read this then I am too near the front

If you can read this then one of us is being carried home!

"If you can read this, that means I didn't put my t-shirt on backwards."

If you could read my mind you wouldn't be smiling...

If you don't believe me, smell my calculator

"If you don't live here, don't surf here!"

If you stare any longer - I may do a somersault

"If you think my front is cute, wait till you see my backside!"

If you tolerate this your tshirt will be next

If you're going to be two faced… at least make one of them pretty

I'll never play as well as this again

I'm a disco dancer

"I'm a modern, independent woman & my priorities are simple… 1 - kids, 2 - tap dancing, 3 - Guinness, 4 - husband (bless him!)"

I'm a pacifist but come Armageddon I'm gonna crack some skulls

I'm a screensaver

I'm a space invader

I'm better looking online

I'm drinking to make you pretty

"I'm gonna have sex with you tonight, so you might as well be there."

I'm here to meet boys

I'm kind of a big deal

I'm not a gynaecologist… but I'll take a look.

I'm not angry… just disappointed.

I'm not as think as you drunk I am…

I'm not being funny but…

I'm not being rude - I'm making noises

I'm not drinking anymore… then again I'm not drinking any less!

"I'm not drunk! I'm naturally loud, clumsy & friendly!"

"I'm not gay, I just like soft furnishings."

I'm not gay. But my girlfriend is!

I'm not lazy… just efficient with my energy

I'm not touching that without gloves and a mask!

"I'm okay; you're okay - in small doses."

I'm pink therefore I'm spam

I'm seriously thinking about getting a dog.

I'm smiling inside

I'm so Emo even my happy meals are sad.

I'm the Irish girl your mother warned you about...

I'm up & dressed - what more do you want!!

I'm what Willis was talking about.

I'm with stupid ->

Imperial storm trooper training academy

"In life, as in art, the beautiful moves in curves"

Instant human just add beer

Insult by association

Insult me to my face!

Is Dave there?

"Is it hot in here, or is it just my heat-vision?"

It might get ugly

It doesn't say what you thought it was going to say

It's 5:50 a.m… do you know where your stack pointer is?

"It's because of you, that people like me are on medication."

"Its immoral, it's illegal, it's unhealthy but I like it!"

It's my hen weekend… but am I bothered though?

10

J - K

Jack Bauer wouldn't stand for this shit!!

Jesus mafia

Jesus saves!!!! (But Cahill taps in the rebound)

"Jesus saves, Buddha does incremental backups"

John Doe

Just because you have one does not mean you should act like one

"Just divorced. We were incompatible, I'm a Virgo and he's an asshole"

Just enough to break the ice... My name's Matt

"Just remember, once you're over the hill you begin to pick up speed."

Kill the last romantic

Kim Wilde has sold a lot of records… and also a lot of gardening books

Kiss me - I'm yours for keeps

Kiss me… I play bass!

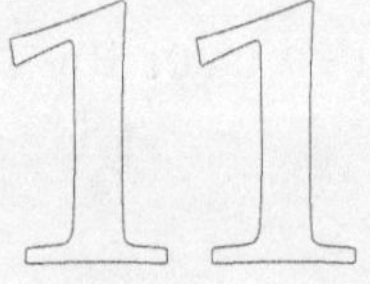

L

Ladies and gentlemen… lets play darts

Leave me alone I'm hung-over!!!!!!!

Leave the chocolate alone and nobody gets hurt

"Left handed "freaks" make beautiful friends x x"

'Legalise conkers!'

Let me through. I have one shoe!

Let's get me out of this hot tshirt

Life is too short to drink bad wine

Linguists do it with their tongues

Little miss talkative

"Live by the board, die by the board"

Live the dream.

Log a call!

"Look, you can see Wales over there? Oh yes. Is that north or south?"

Love Handel

Love is available here at 100% discount. Just don't expect a refund!

Loving me is as easy as pie

12

M

Mac 100%...!

Mad as a bag of badgers.

Made in Italy

Make tea not war

Married 10 years. I give him 2 beautiful kids and he gives me this! I expected at least new boobs!!!!

Me

Medium metal

Merry New Year!!

"Mmm I've just had a nibble... From tha "happy meal menu of love"

Mortuary technician - my day starts when yours ends

Mothers of teens know why some animals eat their young!

Mr. messy

Mummy says I'm special

"My body is a temple, shoes on the outside"

My boss always has a good day!!

My boyfriend is in a promising local band

My course was harder

My eyes have seen the glory

My friend is a moose

"My other shirt is funnier, but it's dirty..."

My other t-shirt is green

My phone's on vibrate for you but still I never ever feel from you

"My, we've been a bit careless, haven't we?"

13

N

Nah then mardy bum

Nan you're a window shopper

Never underestimate the heart of a champion

New operating system installed

Nine 'o levels' but not one in common sense

No I can't fix your computer!

No lorries past this point!

No more pudding! Or else you'll pop

No we are not brothers we are sisters!

"No, I will not loan you 48p for the bus fare home. Get a job."

Nookie in Newquay

Normal service resumed

Not the full ticket!

Now show me... Sand of ass

Numbers are my friends

Nuttier than a squirrel turd

Nymphomaniac treatment centre – staff

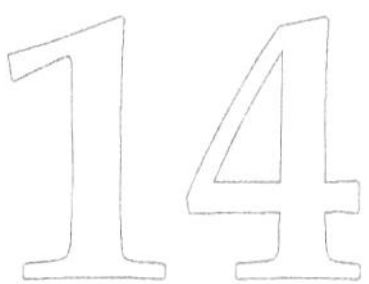

O

Objection!

Official kilt inspector

Ofsteded in England and I passed!

Older than Jesus

Omg I stood him up again!

One in the oven

One more round!

Only losers have hoodies made for their holidays

Oopsi-daisy

Oscar winner

Our character is what we do when we think no-one is looking.

"Our lager, which art in barrels, hallowed be thy drink. Thy will be drunk, (I will be drunk), at home as in the tavern. Give us this day our foamy head, and forgive us our spillages, as we forgive those who spill against us. And lead us not to incarceration, but deliver us from hangovers. For thine is the beer, the bitter and the lager. Forever and ever, barmen"

Outgoing introvert

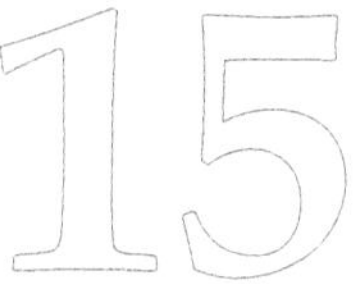

P

P.I.M.P.

P.t.o.

Pain is weakness leaving the body

Palatial elegance

Penguin warden

Pig wrestler

"Pizza sucks, burgers rule!"

Plain clothes cop

Please ignore my magnificent breasts

Please wait. Analogy pending...

"Pressure? That's for tyres, mate"

Probably the best bricklayer in South Wales

Profound and/or witty comment

Proud to be ginger

Psychos never flush

Pull my string to hear me talk…

Put da lime in de coconut and drink dem boad up!

Put the lotion in the basket

16

Q - R

Q: how do make a blonde's eyes twinkle? A: shine a torch in their ear.

Reading this you don't notice my ears

"Real athletes row, all the others just play games"

Resistance is futile. (If <1 ohm)

Respect my authority

"Ride 'em, cowboy!"

Rude

17

S

Same shirt different day!

Save Ferris

"Save your breath, you'll need it to blow up your date!!"

"Saw it, wanted it, threw a tantrum, got it"

"Seriously, could I get any better?!"

Sex & drugs & sausage rolls

She does it by voodoo

She got soul

Shezmiester general

Sleeping to dream about you

Slogan

Smile if you want to sleep with me

"Smile, I know you don't like me"

Smoke me a kipper I'll be back for breakfast

"So much chocolate, so little time!"

So you wanna be a gangster?

Some people see things as they are and say why… but I dream things that never were and ask why not!

"Sotally tober, starkle starkle little twink, who the hell you are I think, I'm not under what you call, the alcofluence of incohol. I'm just a little slort of sheep, I'm not drunk like tinkle peep, I don't know who is me yet, but the drunker I stand here, the longer I get. Just give me one more drink to fill me cup, 'cuz I got all day sober to Sunday up."

Soulville

Stage crew

Stole the show

"Stop the mugging, start the hugging"

Su-per-fine

T

Take out a SLA with me tonight!

Tell your boobs to stop staring at my eyes!

Tell your boyfriend I said thanks

"Thanks for the offer, but I'll make my own way home."

That would be an ecumenical matter

That's enough about you… now let's talk about me!

That's just how I roll

That's Papa Smurf to you!!

"That's right, the Bolshevik revolution was started by leprechauns… little, communist leprechauns"

The band's not too loud - the singers are too quiet

"The chances of anything coming from mars are a million to one, he said… but still they come"

The innocent joy of monkeys on stilts!

The man in the green hat. He is the one… don't believe his lies.

The more people I meet… the more I love my dog!

The mouse did it

"The name's Maximus, I'll have a calzone, shaken not stirred"

The older I get the better I was

The only way to get rid of a temptation is to yield to it

The owls are not what they seem.

The revolution is just a t-shirt away

The world needs more left-handed guitarists!

"There are four basic food groups: milk chocolate, dark chocolate, white chocolate and chocolate truffles."

There's a hurricane called Joy and I'm breakdancin' in the eye

There's no place like 127.0.0.1

"Things you can see from space...The Great Wall of China, the oceans and my hair!"

This girl runs on pint power

This is what a feminist looks like

This is what I call a target rich environment

This shirt is on back to front

This speed is normal for me!

This t-shirt is blue with white writing!

Those aren't pillows!!!

Tig ole bitties

"Title: alpha geek. Definition: the head geek or geek's geek. When no one else knows the answer, or several techno-types give conflicting advise, or the error message says "consult your administrator" and you *are* the administrator, you ask the alpha geek."

Today I decided to wear a yellow t-shirt…

"Too many freaks, not enough circuses!!"

"Triathlete - eating, drinking, singing"

"True friends r hard to find, difficult to leave & impossible to forget"

Truly madly deeply insatiable

T-shirt wearing anorak

53

Tw@

T-shirt wearing anorak

19

U - V

Unexpectedly re-available due to timewaster

Urban fairy

USA's best grandma

USA's super pops.

Viva la cheese-eating surrender monkeys

Von pigeonstein

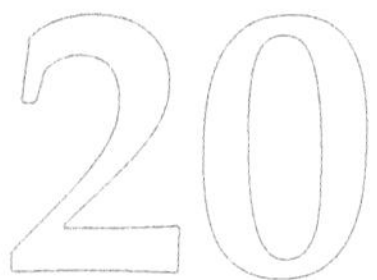

W

Warning!!! This shirt may contain an Irish

Warning!!! This product may contain nuts

Wassup??

Watta guy!!!

We don't need no stinkin' badgers!

Weak knees

Well whoopy shit!!

Well it's not going to suck itself

Well you gotta take advantage...

We're only friends!!

What about the sausages?

What if the hokey cokey really is what it's all about...?

What's that done to the graph?

"What's the crack for tonight like?? Oooh, that's a bit special!!"

What's the use of happiness? It can't buy you money.

"When a ball dreams, it dreams it's a Frisbee"

When god made me he was just showing off

When I think about you I touch my elf...

"When in doubt, make tea"

When it's sunny... I go topless

When this bloody chemo's finished I'm off to Florida!

Which way is starboard?

Who invented the skip?

Who needs big tits when you've got an arse like this?

Who's the granddaddy?

"Why are you reading this, my eyes are up there!"

Why does the nutter always sit next to me?

Why?

Whydoeseveryonealwayspickonthefatboy??

Will code html for food

Will sing for food

Will someone just think of the squirrels??!!

Will work for gin

"Will Young, what a waste."

"Win "Rocky" win"

"Without data, you are just one more person with an opinion"

Witness protection program

Working class hero

Would you like a free blood pressure test?

Wouldn't it be funny if we all worshipped sharks?

"Wow, I love myself to an extreme, and I'm sure you can see why!"

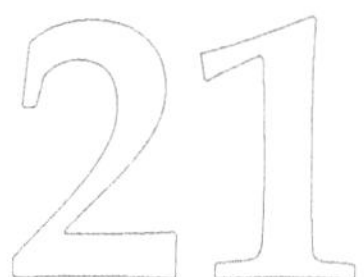

X - Y - Z

"Yes please. White, no sugar"

Yes I have been busy

"Yes ladies, I am the son of one of England's top 10 civil engineers"

"Yes that is a bong in my pocket....and no, I'm not happy to see you!"

Yes you're right... it's all my fault

You are my sunshine

You are not Akeem

You don't need eyes to see… you need vision

"You laugh because I'm different; I laugh because you're all the same"

You looked better on Myspace

You may take my gun but only if you prise it from my cold dead hands

You mess with my muck heap… I mess in your boots!

You probably don't recognise me without my cape…

You say psycho like it's a bad thing

You should have been here yesterday!

You think I look good in this? You should see my other costumes!

"You, me, car park, now"

"Young, willing and more than able!"

Your emails are now safe

61

Your face is a full stop

Your mum says I look fit in this hoodie…

Your point caller?

Your village called… they want their idiot back!

You're not the boss of me now!

You're rather attractive for a beautiful girl with a great body.